Instant jQuery Selectors

Learn how to master the art of effectively using jQuery's selectors

Aurelio De Rosa

BIRMINGHAM - MUMBAI

Instant JQuery Selectors

First published: August 2013

Production Reference: 1230813

Published by Packt Publishing Ltd.
Livery Place
35 Livery Street
Birmingham B3 2PB, UK.

ISBN 978-1-78328-221-0

www.packtpub.com

Credits

Author

Aurelio De Rosa

Reviewers

Kent C. Dodds

Acquisition Editor

Nikhil Karkal

Mary Jasmine Nadar

Commissioning Editor

Nikhil Chinnari

Technical Editor

Dipika Gaonkar

Project Coordinator

Esha Thakker

Proofreader

Joel T. Johnson

Production Coordinator

Adonia Jones

Cover Work

Adonia Jones

Cover Image

Abhinash Sahu

About the Author

Aurelio De Rosa is an Italian web and application developer with more than five years' experience in programming for web using HTML5, CSS3, JavaScript, and PHP. He mainly uses the LAMP stack and frameworks, such as jQuery, jQuery Mobile, and Cordova (PhoneGap). His interests also include web security, web accessibility, SEO, and WordPress.

He is currently self-employed working with the cited technologies and is also a regular blogger for several networks (SitePoint, Tuts+, and FlippinAwesome), where he writes articles about the topics he usually works with and more.

You can find more about him at his website `http://www.audero.it`.

First of all, I'd like to thank my parents, Raffaele and Eufemia, because they gave me chance to study and follow this path that I've chosen, and for this I owe them. With all your sacrifices, you allowed me to have everything a person may need in his life. I also want to thank Annarita for teaching me the true meaning of the word "love". With you my life is full of moments of joy and I hope we'll be together for the rest of our lives. I want to thank Francesco for always being there in the time of need and proving to me that lifetime friendship can really exist.

About the Reviewer

Kent C. Dodds is a young and upcoming front end developer. Kent is currently pursuing his Masters in Information Systems Management degree from Brigham Young University in Provo, Utah. Kent anticipates staying on with Domo Technologies Incorporated upon his graduation as an AngularJS front-end developer. Domo Technologies is a start up making huge waves in the Business Intelligence world and Kent looks forward to helping make that wave grow bigger.

Kent was born and raised in Twin Falls, Idaho as the eleventh child of twelve and has always loved spending time with family. Kent grew up loving being productive with computers and his interests have only grown with time.

Kent loves to contribute to the online community and hopes that his StackOverflow, GitHub, and Google+ accounts will provide himself and others opportunities to discover new technologies to improve themselves professionally.

In his spare time, Kent enjoys spending time with his beautiful wife Brooke and their daughter Becca. They are expecting another addition to their little family in December 2013, and on the day of writing this, Kent and Brooke celebrated their second anniversary. Of course, Kent would like to thank Brooke and Becca without whom he would be a lot less happy and a less satisfied person. Kent also enjoys investigating new technologies and building new things to always keep learning.

Feel free to connect with Kent online at `http://kent.doddsfamily.us`.

www.PacktPub.com

Support files, eBooks, discount offers and more

You might want to visit www.PacktPub.com for support files and downloads related to your book.

Did you know that Packt offers eBook versions of every book published, with PDF and ePub files available? You can upgrade to the eBook version at www.PacktPub.com and as a print book customer, you are entitled to a discount on the eBook copy. Get in touch with us at service@packtpub.com for more details.

At www.PacktPub.com, you can also read a collection of free technical articles, sign up for a range of free newsletters and receive exclusive discounts and offers on Packt books and eBooks.

http://PacktLib.PacktPub.com

Do you need instant solutions to your IT questions? PacktLib is Packt's online digital book library. Here, you can access, read and search across Packt's entire library of books.

Why Subscribe?

- ▸ Fully searchable across every book published by Packt
- ▸ Copy and paste, print and bookmark content
- ▸ On demand and accessible via web browser

Free Access for Packt account holders

If you have an account with Packt at www.PacktPub.com, you can use this to access PacktLib today and view nine entirely free books. Simply use your login credentials for immediate access.

In loving memory of my grandmother, Giuseppina.

Table of Contents

Preface

jQuery is a popular JavaScript library designed to simplify the client-side scripting of HTML, widely used by most of the websites on the Internet. It helps you to manipulate elements, and create fancy interactive websites in a very easy way that is compatible with modern and older browsers as well.

Instant jQuery Selectors will take you as a beginner and turn you into an expert that knows all of the tips and tricks of the pros about the jQuery's basic element: selectors. Through the use of examples, you'll be able to start using selectors efficiently and easily to solve your day-to-day problems.

What this book covers

Setting up jQuery (Must know) explains how to download and include jQuery in a web page and a good rule of thumb to choose between the two major jQuery branches, 1.X and 2.X.

The All selector (Must know) covers the All (or Universal) selector, to select all of the elements of a document.

Selecting by ID (Must know) introduces the ID selector and how jQuery manages it behind the scenes.

Selecting by class (Must know) describes the Class selector and how to optimize it for older browsers.

Selecting by tag (Must know) demonstrates the use of the Element selector and how you can use it in conjunction with other selectors.

Multiple selectors at once (Should know) shows how to use more than one selector in a single call.

Selecting by hierarchy (Must know) covers the hierarchy operators that allow you to retrieve elements by their relationship in the DOM.

Selecting by attributes (Should know) describes how many and what are the selectors to collect elements by their attributes.

Selecting by position using filters (Should know) introduces filters, and in particular those that allow to filter a collection using the elements' positions inside the collection itself.

Selecting from elements using filters (Should know) covers filters specific to form elements.

Child filters (Should know) describes filters to target node's children.

Other filters (Become an expert) shows the filters not covered in the previous recipes.

Custom filters (Become an expert) explains how to create a custom filter using two approaches.

Context matters (Should know) shows how to use the second parameter of the jQuery constructor in order to improve performance.

Improving performance re-using selected elements (Become an expert) demonstrates how to store a collection of previously selected elements in a variable for a later processing and how this method can improve performances.

Methods to filter collections (Become an expert) covers how many and what are the jQuery's methods to filter a collection.

Traversing DOM SubTrees (Become an expert) describes how many and what are the methods that can be applied to a collection, to find elements starting from a matched set.

How to have efficient selectors (Become an expert) explains tips and tricks to improve the performances of a website by simply selecting elements in the right way.

What you need for this book

This book assumes the reader to have a basic understanding of HTML and CSS. In addition, having basic knowledge of JavaScript, its syntax, and some concepts like anonymous functions, events, DOM and callbacks would be beneficial.

Who this book is for

The book is for web developers who want to delve into jQuery, the most popular and adopted JavaScript framework, from its very starting point: selectors. Even if you're already familiar with the framework and its selectors, you could find several tips and tricks that you aren't aware of, especially about performance and how jQuery acts behind the scenes.

Conventions

In this book, you will find a number of styles of text that distinguish between different kinds of information. Here are some examples of these styles, and an explanation of their meaning.

Code words in text are shown as follows: "We can include other contexts through the use of the `include` directive."

A block of code is set as follows:

```
<!DOCTYPE html>
<html>
    <head>
        <meta charset="UTF-8">
        <title>Instant jQuery Selector How-to</title>
    </head>
    <body>
    </body>
</html>
```

When we wish to draw your attention to a particular part of a code block, the relevant lines or items are set in bold:

```
<script src="jquery-1.10.1.min.js"></script>
    <script>
        $(document).ready(function() {
            $('*').css('border', '2px solid #000000');
        });
    </script>
```

New terms and **important words** are shown in bold. Words that you see on the screen, in menus or dialog boxes for example, appear in the text like this: "clicking the **Next** button moves you to the next screen".

 Warnings or important notes appear in a box like this.

 Tips and tricks appear like this.

Reader feedback

Feedback from our readers is always welcome. Let us know what you think about this book—what you liked or may have disliked. Reader feedback is important for us to develop titles that you really get the most out of.

To send us general feedback, simply send an e-mail to feedback@packtpub.com, and mention the book title via the subject of your message.

If there is a topic that you have expertise in and you are interested in either writing or contributing to a book, see our author guide on www.packtpub.com/authors.

Customer support

Now that you are the proud owner of a Packt book, we have a number of things to help you to get the most from your purchase.

Downloading the example code

You can download the example code files for all Packt books you have purchased from your account at http://www.packtpub.com. If you purchased this book elsewhere, you can visit http://www.packtpub.com/support and register to have the files e-mailed directly to you.

Errata

Although we have taken every care to ensure the accuracy of our content, mistakes do happen. If you find a mistake in one of our books—maybe a mistake in the text or the code—we would be grateful if you would report this to us. By doing so, you can save other readers from frustration and help us improve subsequent versions of this book. If you find any errata, please report them by visiting http://www.packtpub.com/submit-errata, selecting your book, clicking on the **errata submission form** link, and entering the details of your errata. Once your errata are verified, your submission will be accepted and the errata will be uploaded on our website, or added to any list of existing errata, under the Errata section of that title. Any existing errata can be viewed by selecting your title from http://www.packtpub.com/support.

Piracy

Piracy of copyright material on the Internet is an ongoing problem across all media. At Packt, we take the protection of our copyright and licenses very seriously. If you come across any illegal copies of our works, in any form, on the Internet, please provide us with the location address or website name immediately so that we can pursue a remedy.

Please contact us at copyright@packtpub.com with a link to the suspected pirated material.

We appreciate your help in protecting our authors, and our ability to bring you valuable content.

Questions

You can contact us at questions@packtpub.com if you are having a problem with any aspect of the book, and we will do our best to address it.

1

Instant jQuery Selectors

Welcome to *Instant jQuery Selectors*. jQuery is a popular JavaScript library, created by John Resig, designed to simplify the client side scripting of HTML. This book will introduce you to the available selectors of this framework. Through the use of examples, you'll be able to start using selectors efficiently and easily to solve your day-to-day problems.

The structure of this book is conceived to help you through the learning process. In fact, the initial recipes will give you an overview of the basic topics, showing you the most commonly used selectors. Conversely, the later recipes will show you how to become a pro by describing more advanced topics such as, creating your own selectors and how to improve the performance of your scripts by just paying attention on how to select elements.

Setting up jQuery (Must know)

This first section will describe how to download and include jQuery in a web page and a good rule of thumb to choose between the two major jQuery branches, 1.X and 2.X, depending on the browsers you need to support. In addition, we'll discuss the benefits of using a **Content Delivery Network** (**CDN**) rather than hosting a local version of the library.

Getting ready

Before we start, we need to download the jQuery library. To do that, simply visit `http://jquery.com/download/` and get the latest version of the 1.X branch. At the time of writing, the last release is 1.10.1. The name of the file typically has the form `jquery-VERSION.js`, so your downloaded file should be named as `jquery-1.10.1.js`.

Now, open your favorite text editor or IDE and let's type some markup. If you don't know what to choose, a simple text editor should be enough. On Windows, a good and free one is Notepad++, on Linux you can use gEdit or Nano, and on Mac you can use Sublime Text.

How to do it...

To set up your first web page that uses jQuery, perform the following steps:

1. Create a folder and name it as you prefer, for example `code`.

2. Create an HTML file inside it and name it `template.html`. Then, put the previously downloaded jQuery library, `jquery-1.10.1.js`, into the `code` folder too.

3. Now, we need to write a basic template that we'll use throughout the rest of the book. So, open the `template.html` file with your editor of choice and write the following code:

```
<!DOCTYPE html>
<html>
    <head>
        <meta charset="UTF-8">
        <title>Instant jQuery Selectors</title>
    </head>
    <body>
    </body>
</html>
```

Downloading the example code

You can download the example code files for all Packt books you have purchased from your account at http://www.packtpub.com. If you purchased this book elsewhere, you can visit http://www.packtpub.com/support and register to have the files e-mailed directly to you.

4. With the template in place, we need to include jQuery. To do that, simply add the highlighted line wherever you want inside the <head> tag. I'll put it just after the <title>:

```
...
<title>Instant jQuery Selectors How-to</title>
<script src="jquery-1.10.1.js"></script>
</head>
...
```

5. Save the file.

There's more...

Although simple, the previous steps give us several points to discuss.

What version to use?

As I said, at the time of writing, jQuery has two major branches under development from which to choose. What version to pick really depends on where you're using the framework and what browsers you intend to support.

jQuery 1.X supports all of the versions of Chrome, Firefox, Safari, Opera, and Internet Explorer starting from version 6. The new version, instead, dropped the support for Internet Explorer 6, 7, and 8 in exchange for a smaller size and better performance. This means that if you see a web page that relies on jQuery 2.X using Internet Explorer 8, the script will fail.

So, what version should you use? Here are some use cases:

- In case you're developing a website where you need to target an audience as wide as possible (for example, an institutional website), you should use version 1.X.

- If you're developing a website that doesn't need to support older versions of Internet Explorer (for example, if it runs in a controlled environment such as, a company local network), you can use jQuery 2.X.

- If you're developing a mobile app using **PhoneGap**, or similar frameworks, you don't need to support Internet Explorer 6 to 8. So, you can safely use jQuery 2.X.

 Based on the StatCounter June 2013 statistics (`http://gs.statcounter.com/#browser_version_partially_combined-ww-monthly-201306-201306-bar`), Internet Explorer 6 has a market share of approximately 0.3 percent, IE7 has approximately 0.5 percent, and IE8 has approximately 8 percent. So, before choosing your jQuery version, think twice about your targeted audience.

Compressed or not?

On the jQuery website you could note that for each release (for example, 1.10.1) there is also a compressed (sometimes called "minified") version. The difference between the normal and the minified versions is that the former is intended for the development stage, while the latter for the production stage. In fact, the compressed version not only removes the useless spaces but also shrinks variables' name making it hard to read and debug your code that relies on the library. On the other hand, the advantage of a compressed library is the reduction in size of the script that leads to bandwidth savings for the end users.

Using a CDN

In the previous steps, we've included a local hosted copy of the library, but we can also rely on **Content Delivery Network** (**CDN**). A CDN is a distributed system of servers created to serve contents to end users with high availability and performance at a great speed. So, using a CDN to load jQuery, we can speed up the loading process because being on a different host, the loading parallelism increases, and since a lot of websites use CDNs, there's a higher probability that the required framework version is already in the user's browser cache. There are several CDNs you can use but the most famous ones are the jQuery CDN (`http://code.jquery.com`) and the Google CDN (`https://developers.google.com/speed/libraries/devguide`).

For example, using the jQuery CDN to include the same version seen before, you can write the following code:

```
<script src="http://code.jquery.com/jquery-1.10.1.js"></script>
```

If you want to include the compressed version instead, you should write the following code:

```
<script src="http://code.jquery.com/jquery-1.10.1.min.js"></script>
```

Now that you know how to use a CDN, there's a fact you should be aware of. On the Internet, no server or network has a 100 percent uptime. This means that in some situations, although rather rare, a CDN network can be down or not accessible. If this happens, your website's code that relies on the framework will stop working. To avoid this issue, there's a smart solution you can learn and use, also adopted by the people behind HTML5 boilerplate (`http://html5boilerplate.com`). The idea is to request a copy of the framework from a CDN and check if it has been loaded and test whether the jQuery property of the `window` object is defined. If the test fails, a code that will load a local hosted copy is injected. The reason for the test is that once loaded, jQuery adds the jQuery property mentioned that exposes all of the framework's methods. Moreover, the library adds an additional property that is a reference to the jQuery property called `$`, acting as a shortcut. They are exactly the same object as you can see in the following code taken from the jQuery source:

```
// Expose jQuery to the global object
window.jQuery = window.$ = jQuery;
```

In conclusion, since the local copy is in a folder called `js`, the following code implements this idea:

```
<script src="http://ajax.googleapis.com/ajax/libs/jquery/1.10.1/
jquery.min.js"></script>
<script>window.jQuery || document.write('<script src="js/jquery-
1.10.1.min.js"><\/script>')</script>
```

As a final note, I want to highlight that using a CDN in a page that doesn't run on a web server could cause an error on some browsers.

The All selector (Must know)

With our template in place, we can start diving into the world of jQuery selectors. A selector is a string that allows you to retrieve DOM's elements. The first selector we'll look at is the `All` (or Universal) selector. We'll use it to apply a border to all of the page's elements.

How to do it...

To achieve our goal, perform the following steps:

1. Create a copy of the `template.html` file and rename it `the-all-selector.html`.

2. Inside the `<body>` tag, add the following HTML markup:

   ```html
   <h1>The all selector</h1>
     <div>
        This example shows how to use the All selector.
        <p>As you can see, it doesn't matter we're different tags, we
   all have the border applied.</p>
        <span>Every tag has the border, even the body, the html and
   the head tag!</span>
     </div>
   ```

3. Edit the `<head>` section of the page by adding the following highlighted code:

   ```html
   <script src="jquery-1.10.1.min.js"></script>
   <script>
       $(document).ready(function() {
           $('*').css('border', '2px solid #000000');
       });
   </script>
   </head>
   ```

4. Save the file and open it with your favorite browser.

How it works...

In step 2, we put some elements inside the `<body>` tag to have something to work with but there isn't anything special here.

Then, we created a new `<script>` tag where we wrote our JavaScript instructions. To call the jQuery methods, we used the $ property for brevity. It's important to add the script after the jQuery file, otherwise our code won't work because we can't use the jQuery methods before the library is loaded.

The first method used, although a little bit hidden, is the constructor. This method accepts up to two arguments and, depending on their number and type, performs different tasks. Just like other several jQuery's methods, it allows for **chaining**, a programming technique that lets you call several methods in a single statement. Although not restricted to this, its most common use is to select elements retrieved from the **DOM (Document Object Model)**. In this case, it accepts two parameters, a selector and optionally a context, and returns a jQuery object containing a collection of DOM elements that match the given criteria. In our task, we used the `document` object as a selector and then called the `ready()` method relying on chaining.

> For the sake of brevity, I'll use returns a collection to intend a jQuery object containing a collection from now on.

The `ready()` method called on the `document` object is one of the most common statements by programmers using this library. It accepts as its only argument a function that will be executed when the ready event is fired, and that is as soon as the DOM is fully loaded. This means that inside the handler passed to `ready()` you can safely access all of the elements of your page. In the example shown, we've used an anonymous function but we can also define a function and then pass just the function's name.

Inside our handler we have just one statement. The first part is a call to the jQuery constructor that we've just analyzed. This time, however, we used one of the selectors available, the `All` selector. It's represented by an asterisk (`*`) and should be familiar to you if you're experienced with CSS. This choice is not casual and, as we'll discover in the next chapters, it's a frequent pattern to adopt the same convention used in CSS. As the name says, it asks jQuery to pick up all of the DOM elements of your page, even the `<head>` element and its children.

After we've selected all of the elements, we called the `css()` function to apply a 2px width, solid and black (#000000) border to the matched elements. Hence, the border is really set to all of the elements on the page, as proven by the following screenshot made using the Google Chrome developer tools:

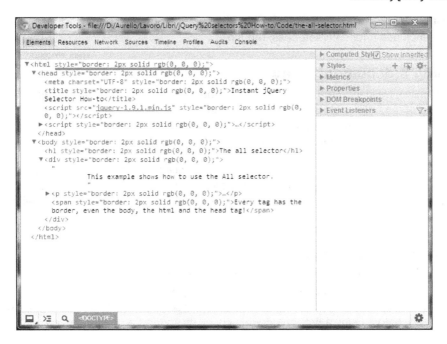

`css()` accepts up to two arguments and the first is usually a CSS property name. If you pass a string with a CSS property, the method gets the value for the first element in the set of matched elements. If you pass a CSS property and a value, as we did in the recipe, the method acts on each element matched. Note that it can also accept an object as its first parameter to set more properties at once.

There's more...

Like the previous section, this short recipe gives us some points to discuss.

Alternatives to $(document).ready()

We have two more ways to call the `ready()` function on the document object. The first and shorter one is to write `$(handler)`. So, if we want to rewrite our recipe using this syntax, it becomes:

```
$(function() {
    $('*').css('border', '2px solid #000000');
});
```

Another equivalent way is to write `$().ready(handler)`. Thus, our code turns into:

```
$().ready(function() {
    $('*').css('border', '2px solid #000000');
});
```

This syntax is not recommended by the official documentation and, honestly, I've never seen it used. I've included it for completeness, though.

Avoiding $(document).ready()

In our example, we loaded the jQuery library and our script inside the `<head>` tag. Doing so, the loading of the page is blocked until they're completely loaded and the users won't see anything of your page. Therefore, it's better to put them just before the closing tag of body element. In this way, you'll enhance the experience of your users.

I chose to put it inside the `<head>` tag to have the chance to explain `$(document).ready`, but keep in mind that by having your scripts at the bottom of the page you can completely avoid the use of `$(document).ready`. In fact, at that point, all of the other elements are already in the DOM.

css() and browsers support

The CSS styles applied with the `css()` function are dependent on the browser's support. So, if the latter doesn't support a property you set, it simply won't work as you expected. In fact, jQuery doesn't try to overcome the limitations of a browser's style rendering with the exception of opacity. So, before using a property double-check its support among browsers.

Selectors and browsers support

Unlike the `css()` method, whatever selector you'll pass to jQuery, chosen among those covered in this book and listed at `http://api.jquery.com/category/selectors/`, it'll return the expected elements' collection regardless of the browsers support. Thus, we can use them all without worries, jQuery will watch our back.

Performance

The use of the universal selector is highly discouraged due to its bad performance. Using it, jQuery needs to traverse and select all of the DOM's nodes and, with a huge number of elements, the process is very slow. Moreover, we've seen that it retrieves elements that aren't really needed to achieve the desired goal, like the `<head>` tag.

Having said that, in those situations where you'll really need to retrieve all of the elements inside a node, you can always replace it in favor of the use of other methods, such as `children()` and `find()`, that usually lead to better performance.

Selecting by ID (Must know)

In this section we'll learn how to select an element by its ID and apply the same border seen previously.

How to do it...

This task can be achieved by performing the following instructions:

1. Create a copy of the `template.html` file and rename it as `selecting-by-id.html`.

2. Inside the `<body>` tag, add the following HTML markup:

```
<h1 id="title">The Id selector</h1>
<div id="container">
    This example shows you how to use the Id selector.
    <p id="description">As you can see, this time the border is
applied only to the h1 element because of its id.</p>
    <span id="note">Hey, I'm a note</span>
</div>
```

3. Edit the `<head>` section as we did in the previous chapter, but this time add this script after the jQuery library instead:

```
<script>
    $(document).ready(function() {
        $('#title').css('border', '2px solid #000000');
    });
</script>
```

4. Save the file and open it with your favorite browser.

How it works...

The code shown is very similar to the previous code, but for the purpose of the task, we've applied an id to all of the elements children of `<body>`. Also, the texts have changed, but this is much less important.

The core part of our code is the third step where, instead of the All selector, we've used the ID selector. In our example, we've used it to pick up the `<h1>` having as id `title` and then apply the border. The ID selector is characterized by the sign # prepended to the value of the element's ID attribute and using it, jQuery returns a collection of either zero or one DOM element. It's important to highlight that this selector is surely the fastest one, regardless of the browser used since when it turns to deal with an ID, behind the scenes jQuery uses the JavaScript function `document.getElementById()`, which is very efficient.

Remember that, although doable, having more than one element with the same ID is invalid and must be avoided. However, in case you decided to ignore this rule (Please don't! Really!), be aware that jQuery will retrieve only the first matched element encountered. Moreover, just like the other selectors that we'll see, when no match is found, an empty collection is returned.

There's more...

There are many characters you can use to set the ID of your elements, but you need to be aware that some of them need to be treated carefully.

Escaping special characters

The value of an ID doesn't allow just alphabetical characters, but also: dots, hyphens, semicolons, and others as regulated by the W3C (http://www.w3.org/TR/html4/types.html#type-id). You are free to use each of the described characters, but to tell jQuery to treat these characters literally rather than as CSS notation they must be escaped. You can escape them by prepending them with two backslashes.

So, if we want to select an element having ID .title, we would have to write $('#\\.title').

Storing a collection

Once you performed a selection, the matched collection of elements can be stored in a variable for a later processing. The usual convention to name these variables is to write a dollar sign in front of the variable's name to highlight that it contains a jQuery object. Here is a example:

```
var $title = $('#title');
var $borderedTitle = $('#title').css('border', '2px solid #000000');
```

Selecting by class (Must know)

In this recipe we'll see how to select a collection of elements using the Class selector. Our goal is to hide all of the elements having the class red.

How to do it...

To achieve the prefixed objective, we need to perform the following steps:

1. Create a copy of the template.html file and rename it as selecting-by-class.html.

2. Inside the `<body>` tag, add the following HTML markup:

```html
<h1 id="title" class="bold red">The Class selector</h1>
<div id="container">
    This example shows you how to use the Class selector.
    <p id="description" class="red">After you'll click the button
below, the h1 and this p will be hidden.</p>
    <p id="note" class="green">This happens because of their class
attribute's value.</p>
</div>
<button id="hide-button">Hide elements!</button>
```

3. Edit the `<head>` section of the page adding this code:

```html
<script>
    $(document).ready(function() {
        $('#hide-button').click(function() {
            $('.red').hide();
        });
    });
</script>
```

4. Save the file and open it with your favorite browser.

How it works...

First of all, we need to write some markup to fill the web page. Most of the added elements have a class attribute defined with some hypothetical values. Those classes don't actually change the style because we haven't defined them. One of the tags written is a button that we'll use to attach a handler.

Inside our usual anonymous function, attached to the document's ready event, we put our logic. Using the knowledge gained so far, we select the button by its ID (hide button), and then attach another anonymous function that will be fired as soon as a click event occurs. In general, this event is triggered when the mouse is over an element, and then the mouse button is pressed and released. In our case, we're listening when this happens to the button. Inside the inner handler, we have just one statement.

Using the CSS conventions, we're prepending a dot before the chosen class name, red. So, we're passing the string to the jQuery constructor to select all of the elements having class red. The framework won't choose only the nodes having red as unique value of the class attribute (for example, `class="red"`), but also those having multiple classes where one of them is red (for example, `class="bold red"`). Giving the HTML code written, the selected elements are the h1 and the first p.

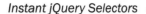

Once we have retrieved the collection, we pass it to the library's `hide()` method. As the name suggests, it hides the matched elements. It's highly configurable, but for the sake of our example, we used its most basic form that hides elements immediately, without animation.

There's more...

Several browsers have a native function to select elements by their class name. Let's see what jQuery does behind the scenes.

getElementsByClassName()

Where possible, jQuery uses the `getElementsByClassName()` function to select elements using their class name. The browsers where this function is applied are IE9+, Firefox 3+, Chrome, Safari, and Opera 9.5+. Being native, its performances are quite good, although not comparable to those of `getElementById()`.

 Versions of Internet Explorer prior to 9 don't have a native function to select elements by a class, so with a considerable amount of elements in the DOM, the performance can be very bad. However, for projects that aren't targeting IE6 to 8 users, or are using jQuery 2.X, this note can be ignored.

In case you need to take care of performances for Internet Explorer 6 to 8, here is a tip for you.

Due to the lack of `getElementsByClassName()` in IE6 to 8 you can optimize the search by class name, if it's applied to elements with the same tag name, prepending the latter to the class name itself. For example, if you want to select all of the `p` having class `red`, instead of using `$('.red')`, you can write `$('p.red')`.

Selecting elements having two or more classes

In the last example, we've seen how to select elements having `red` as class, but you can do more than that. You can also select elements having a class and another one. For example, suppose we want to select an element with both `red` and `bold` class. To achieve this goal, you need to simply concatenate class selectors, as follows:

```
$('.red.bold').hide();
```

Selecting by tag (Must know)

In this recipe, you'll learn how to select elements by their tag name using what is known as element selector. The goal of this task is to show you how to select and hide the paragraphs in the page.

How to do it...

To achieve our goal, perform the following the steps:

1. Create a copy of the `template.html` file and rename it as `selecting-by-tag-names.html`.

2. Inside the `<body>` tag, add the following HTML markup:

```html
<h1>The Tag name selector</h1>
<div>
    This example shows you how to use a tag name.
    <p>After you'll click the button below, both the paragraph of
this page will be hidden.</p>
    <p>I'm yet another paragraph</p>
</div>
<button id="hide-button">Hide elements!</button>
```

3. Edit the `<head>` section of the page adding this code:

```html
<script>
    $(document).ready(function() {
        $('#hide-button').click(function() {
            $('p').hide();
        });
    });
</script>
```

4. Save the file and open it with your favorite browser.

How it works...

Although the entire recipe is slightly different from the previous one, it acts differently. As usual, before typing some JavaScript, we set up a short content for our page.

Once the markup is in place, we wrote the listener for the `document.ready` event and the click event on the button. Inside the latter, we used the jQuery constructor and passed it a tag name. I chose to hide the two paragraphs, but you can replace it with the tag you prefer. Unlike the other selectors we've seen so far, to collect elements by their tag name, we don't need to add any additional character (as we do in CSS). Thus, to hide the paragraphs, we just pass p to the constructor and then call the `hide()` function.

There's more...

Tag names can be combined with other selectors. Let's learn how.

Selecting and using tag names with classes and IDs

The Element selector can be used in conjunction with class and ID selectors to restrict the retrieved collection by just prepending them. For example, we can ask jQuery to hide all of the paragraphs having class `red`. To do that, we can write the following code:

```
$('p.red').hide();
```

Another example is to use a tag name with an ID. For example we can select the paragraph having as its ID `description`, as follows:

```
$('p#description').hide();
```

In such cases, jQuery performs a supplementary test before identifying the element as a match. Therefore, it'll retrieve the first (if any) paragraph having ID description. Recalling what I pointed out in the *Selecting by ID (Must know)* recipe, you should never need to use the tag name with the ID selector since you should have just one element with a given ID.

getElementsByTagName()

Where possible, jQuery uses `getElementsByTagName()` to select elements using their tag name. This function is widely supported by all of the major browsers, including Internet Explorer starting from version 6 with full support and 5.5 with partial support.

Multiple selectors at once (Should know)

This section will teach you how to use more than one selector, and it doesn't matter if they're of the same or different kind, in a single call. The goal of the task is to print on the console the length of the retrieved collections.

How to do it...

This task can be achieved by performing the following instructions:

1. Create a copy of the `template.html` file and rename it as `multiple-selectors-at-once.html`.

2. Inside the `<body>` tag, add the following HTML markup:

```
<h1 id="title" class="bold red">Multiple selectors at once</h1>
<div id="container" class="wrapper">
    This example shows you the use of Multiple selector.
    <p id="description" class="red">Using it you'll have better
performance, so adopt it when possible.</p>
    <p id="note" class="green">This is a good note!</p>
</div>
```

```
<div class="wrapper">
    <h2>jQuery is so cool!</h2>
    <p class="red">I'm yet another paragraph</p>
</div>
```

3. Edit the `<head>` section of the page adding this code:

```
<script>
    $(document).ready(function() {
        console.log($('#container, #note').length);
        console.log($('.wrapper, div').length);
        console.log($('p, h1.red, #title').length);
    });
</script>
```

4. Save the file and open it with your favorite browser.

How it works...

So far, we've seen four types of selectors: All, Id, Class, and Element. Now, it's time to see how we can use them in a single selection to apply the same effect or function. In this way, our website will gain in performance because the DOM is traversed only once. Thus, we'll have once traversing for the N used selectors, instead of N traversing, once for each selector.

To see the multiple selectors in action, in the second step, we've added a higher number of elements to the DOM. Some of them have an id, some have a class, others both and others just nothing. This will help us to use selectors of different type and to highlight the power of the multiple selectors.

To use it, we've to just add a comma after our selector. You can see it as the OR logical operator inside an expression. There isn't a limit for the usable selectors, therefore we can use as many of them as we like. Just remember that if an element has more than one match, it's retrieved once. jQuery takes care of wiping out all of the duplicates for us. Moreover, the order of the DOM elements returned may not be identical to our selectors, as they will be collected in order of appearance inside the document.

In the first statement of the anonymous function, we're asking to retrieve all of the elements having either id container or note. Then, we print the size of the collection inside the jQuery object accessing the `length` property. The line `$('#container, #note')` produces 2 as a result because jQuery retrieves `<div id="container" class="wrapper">` and `<p id="note" class="green">`.

The second line requires elements having class wrapper plus all of the `<div>` instances. The first selector matches only `<div id="container" class="wrapper">` while the second matches the two <div> instances of the page. Recalling what you've learned a few moments ago, jQuery will delete all of the duplicates for us. Thus, in this case too the printed value is 2 because one of the two <div> instances appears twice in the collection.

In the third and last statement, we used the Element selector to retrieve all of the paragraphs, the tag name together with the Class selector to retrieve the `<h1>` having class red, and the ID selector to retrieve the element having ID title. If the previous examples were clear enough, it isn't hard to understand that the console will print 4. In fact, the paragraphs found are three, there isn't a match for the second selector and the third picks the only `<h1>` of the page.

Selecting by hierarchy (Must know)

This chapter explains how to combine the selectors seen so far using hierarchy operators to retrieve elements by their relationship in the DOM.

Getting ready

Before we dive into the code, we should be aware of the weapons in our belt. The following is a table describing all of the selectors that belong to this category:

Name	Identifying Character	Syntax	Description
Child	>	Parent > Children (for example, #title > .red)	Selects all direct children "Children" of the parent specified by "Parent".
Descendant	(space)	Ancestor Descendants (for example, .wrapper .red)	Selects all descendants "Descendants" having in their ancestor list "Ancestor".
Next Adjacent	+	Prev + Next (for example. h1 + p)	Selects all "Next" elements that are immediately after a "Prev".
Next Sibling	~	Prev ~ Siblings (for example. .bold ~ p)	Selects all sibling "Siblings" elements that follow (not just immediately after) and have the same parent of "Prev".

Let's look at the steps to perform for this recipe.

How to do it...

To achieve the prefixed goal we need to perform these steps:

1. Create a copy of the `template.html` file and rename it as `hierarchy-selectors.html`.

2. Inside the `<body>` tag, add the following HTML markup:

```html
<h1 id="title" class="bold border">Multiple selectors at once</h1>
<div class="wrapper">
    <h2>A subtitle</h2>
    <p>This demo shows how to combine selectors based on their
relationship.</p>
    <p id="description" class="border">Using it you'll have better
performance, so adopt it when possible.</p>
    <span>This is a sibling span</span>
    <p id="note" class="green">This is a good note!</p>
    <span>This is yet another sibling span</span>
</div>
<div id="content" class="wrapper">
    <h2>jQuery is so cool!</h2>
    <p class="border">I'm yet another paragraph</p>
    <ul>
        <li>The first of the list</li>
        <li>I'm the second, not bad!</li>
        <li>Third list item here</li>
    </ul>
</div>
```

3. Edit the `<head>` section of the page adding this code:

```html
<script>
    $(document).ready(function() {
        $('div > .border').css('border', '2px solid #000000');
        $('#content li').css('color', '#FF0A27');
        $('h2 + p').css('margin-left', '40px');
        $('h2 ~ span').css('background-color', '#ABF9FF');
    });
</script>
```

4. Save the file and open it with your favorite browser. It should look like the following screenshot:

Multiple selectors at once

A subtitle

This demo shows how to combine selectors based on their relationship.

Using it you'll have better performance, so adopt it when possible.

This is a sibling span

This is a good note!

This is yet another sibling span

jQuery is so cool!

I'm yet another paragraph

*   The first of the list
*   I'm the second, not bad!
*   Third list item here

How it works...

This recipe has been built to use all of the discussed hierarchical selectors, so you can easily fix them in your mind. Each of them targets a certain number of nodes and then assigns a style property, helping you in recognizing the selected elements at first glance.

The first statement picks up the elements having class border that are children (or direct descendant) of a `<div>`, that is the nodes that are just one level under their parent. The elements that match this criteria are the second `<p>` of the first `<div>`, and the `<p>` inside the second `<div>`. Once retrieved, we'll apply them a 2px width, solid and black border, as you learned in the *Selecting by ID (Must know)* recipe.

The second selection adopts the Descendant selector to collect all of the descendants, no matter the depth level they are, of those elements that match the first selector. In this specific case, we're choosing all of the `<li>` inside of a `<div>`. The result is a collection containing the list items inside the second `<div>`, to which we set the font color to red using the jQuery's `css()` method.

The third line of code of our anonymous function selects the paragraphs that are just after a subtitle (`<h2>`) and share the same parent. Those elements are moved on the right of 40px using the property margin-left. You can easily recognize them looking at the earlier screenshot.

The last selection of our example chooses all of the `<span>` instances positioned after a subtitle (`<h2>`) and applies a blue background color to them.

Selecting by attributes (Should know)

In this section, we'll see how to select elements by their attributes paying attention to some quirks that can lead to an unexpected behavior.

Getting ready

These selectors are easily recognizable because they are wrapped by square brackets (for example, [selector]). This type of selector is always used coupled with other, like those seen so far, although this can be implicit as we'll see in few moments. In my experience, you'll often use them with the Element selector, but this can vary based on your needs.

How many and what are the selectors of this type? Glad you asked! Here is a table that gives you an overview:

Name	Syntax	Description
Contains	[attribute*="value"] (for example `input[name*="cod"]`)	Selects the elements that have the value specified as a substring of the given attribute.
Contains Prefix	[attribute|="value"] (for example, `a[class|="audero-"]`)	Selects nodes with the given value equal or equal followed by a hyphen inside the specified attribute.
Contains Word	[attribute~="value"] (for example, `span[data-level~="hard"]`)	Selects elements that have the specified attribute with a value equal to or containing the given value delimited by spaces.
Ends With	[attribute$="value"] (for example, `div[class$="wrapper"]`)	Selects nodes having the value specified at the end of the given attribute's value.
Equals	[attribute="value"] (for example, `p[draggable="true"]`)	Selects elements that have the specified attribute with a value equal to the given value delimited by spaces. This selector performs an exact match.
Not Equal	[attribute!="value"] (for example, `a[target!="_blank"]`)	Selects elements that don't have the specified attribute or have it but with a value not equal to the given value delimited by spaces.
Starts With	[attribute^="value"] (for example, `img[alt^="photo"]`)	Selects nodes having the value specified at the start of the given attribute's value.

Name	Syntax	Description
Has	[attribute] (for example, `input[placeholder]`)	Selects elements that have the attribute specified, regardless of its value.

As you've seen in the several examples in the table, we've used all of these selectors with other ones. Recalling what I said few moments ago, sometimes you can have used them with an implicit selector. In fact, take the following example:

```
$('[placeholder]')
```

What's the "hidden" selector? If you guessed All, you can pat yourself on the back. You're really smart! In fact, it's equivalent to write:

```
$('*[placeholder]')
```

How to do it...

There are quite a lot of Attribute selectors, therefore, we won't build an example for each of them, and I'm going to show you two demos. The first will teach you the use of the Attribute Contains Word selector to print on the console the value of the collected elements. The second will explain the use of the Attribute Has selector to print the value of the placeholder's attribute of the retrieved nodes.

Let's write some code!

To build the first example, follow these steps:

1. Create a copy of the `template.html` file and rename it as `contain-word-selector.html`.

2. Inside the `<body>` tag, add the following HTML markup:

```
<h1>Rank</h1>
<table>
    <thead>
        <th>Name</th>
        <th>Surname</th>
        <th>Points</th>
    </thead>
    <tbody>
        <tr>
            <td class="name">Aurelio</td>
            <td>De Rosa</td>
            <td class="highlight green">100</td>
        </tr>
```

```html
<tr>
    <td class="name">Nikhil</td>
    <td>Chinnari</td>
    <td class="highlight">200</td>
</tr>
<tr>
    <td class="name">Esha</td>
    <td>Thakker</td>
    <td class="red highlight void">50</td>
</tr>
</tbody>
</table>
```

3. Edit the `<head>` section adding the following lines just after the `<title>`:

```html
<style>
    .highlight {
        background-color: #FF0A27;
    }
</style>
```

4. Edit the `<head>` section of the page adding this code:

```html
<script>
    $(document).ready(function() {
        var $elements = $('table td[class~="highlight"]');
        console.log($elements.length);
    });
</script>
```

5. Save the file and open it with your favorite browser.

To create the second example, performs the following steps instead:

1. Create a copy of the `template.html` file and rename it as `has-selector.html`.

2. Inside the `<body>` tag, add the following HTML markup:

```html
<form name="registration-form" id="registration-form"
action="registration.php" method="post">
    <input type="text" name="name" placeholder="Name" />
    <input type="text" name="surname" placeholder="Surname" />
    <input type="email" name="email" placeholder="Email" />
    <input type="tel" name="phone-number" placeholder="Phone
number" />
```

```
            <input type="submit" value="Register" />
            <input type="reset" value="Reset" />
        </form>
```

3. Edit the `<head>` section of the page adding this code:

```
<script>
    $(document).ready(function() {
        var $elements = $('input[placeholder]');
        for(var i = 0; i < $elements.length; i++) {
            console.log($elements[i].placeholder);
        }
    });
</script>
```

4. Save the file and open it with your favorite browser.

How it works...

In the first example, we created a table with four rows, one for the header and three for the data, and three columns. We put some classes to several columns, and in particular, we used the class `highlight`. Then, we set the definition of this class so that an element having it assigned, will have a red background color.

In the next step, we created our usual script (hey, this is still a book on jQuery, isn't it?) where we selected all of the `<td>` having the class `highlight` assigned that are descendants (in this case we could use the Child selector as well) of a `<table>`. Once done, we simply print the number of the collected elements. The console will confirm that, as you can see by yourself loading the page, that the matched elements are three. Well done!

In the second step, we created a little registration form. It won't really work since the backend is totally missing, but it's good for our discussion. As you can see, our form takes advantage of some of the new features of HTML5, like the new `<input>` types `e-mail` and `tel` and the placeholder attribute.

In our usual handler, we're picking up all of the `<input>`instance's in the page having the `placeholder` attribute specified and assigning them to a variable called `$elements`. Recalling what we learned in the *Selecting by id (Must know)* recipe, we're prepending a dollar sign to the variable name to highlight that it stores a jQuery object. With the next block of code, we iterate over the object to access the elements by their index position. Then we log on the console the placeholder's value accessing it using the dot operator. As you can see, we accessed the property directly, without using a method. This happens because the collection's elements are plain DOM elements and not jQuery objects. If you replicated correctly the demo you should see this output in your console:

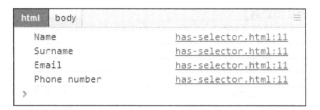

In this recipe, we chose all of the page's <input> instance's, not just those inside the form since we haven't specified it. A better selection would be to restrict the selection using the form's id, that is very fast as we've already discussed. Thus, our selection will turn into:

```
$('#registration-form input[placehoder]')
```

We can have an even better selection using the jQuery's find() method that retrieves the descendants that matches the given selector:

```
$('#registration-form').find('input[placehoder]')
```

There's more...

You can also use more than one attribute selector at once.

Multiple attribute selector

In case you need to select nodes that match two or more criteria, you can use the Multiple Attribute selector. You can chain how many selectors you liked, it isn't limited to two.

Let's say that you want to select all of the <input> instance's of type email and have the placeholder attribute specified, you would need to write:

```
$('input[type="email"][placeholder]')
```

Not equal selector

This selector isn't part of the CSS specifications, so it can't take advantage of the native querySelectorAll() method. The official documentation has a good hint to avoid the problem and have better performance:

 For better performance in modern browsers, use $("your-pure-css-selector").not('[name="value"]') instead.

Using filter() and attr()

jQuery really has a lot of methods to help you in your work and thanks to this, you can achieve the same task in a multitude of ways. While the attribute selectors are important, it can be worth to see how you could achieve the same result seen before using `filter()` and `attr()`.

`filter()` is a function that accepts only one argument that can be of different types, but you'll usually see codes that pass a selector or a function. Its aim is to reduce a collection, iterating over it, and keeping only the elements that match the given parameter. The `attr()` method, instead, accepts up to two arguments and the first is usually an attribute name. We'll use it simply as a getter to retrieve the value of the elements' placeholder.

To achieve our goal, replace the selection instruction with these lines:

```
var $elements = $('#registration-form input').filter(function() {
    return ($(this).attr("placeholder") !== undefined);
});
```

The main difference here is the anonymous function we passed to the `filter()` method. Inside the function, this refers to the current DOM element processed, so to be able to use jQuery's methods we need to wrap the element in a jQuery object. Some of you may guess why we haven't used the plain DOM elements accessing the `placeholder` attribute directly. The reason is that the result won't be the one expected. In fact, by doing so, you'll have an empty string as a value even if the `placeholder` attribute wasn't set for that element making the strict test against `undefined` useless.

Selecting by position using filters (Should know)

This recipe is the first that describes other types of selectors called **filters**. We've already seen some selectors that are based on the relation with other elements, but in this section we'll meet those that are under the filter category.

Getting ready

As the name suggests, these selectors work with other type of selectors, implicitly or explicitly like the attribute ones, to reduce further the set of matched elements. You can easily recognize them because they start with a semicolon sign (`:`). Some of them accept an argument that is passed inside the parentheses. The filters presented in this section help us by reducing elements based on their index inside the collection retrieved (not of the DOM) using the selectors already processed.

The selectors belonging to this category are as follows:

Name	Syntax	Description
Equal to	selector:eq(index) (for example, `div:eq(1)`)	Selects the element that has a position equal to index+1.
Even	selector:even (for example, `li:even`)	Selects all of the even-indexed elements of the retrieved collection.
First	selector:first (for example, `.bold:first`)	Selects just the first element of the set match.
Greater than	selector:gt(index) (for example, `li:gt(3)`)	Selects all of the nodes with a position greater then index+1.
Last	selector:last (for example, `input[class]:last`)	Selects the last element of the retrieved collection.
Less than	selector:lt(index) (for example, `.bold:lt(2)`)	Selects the nodes having position less then index+1.
Odd	selector:odd (for example, `h3:odd`)	Selects odd-indexed elements of the retrieved collection.

Now that you've read these filters, consider this: `:eq`, `:gt`, and `:lt` also accept a negative index. In that case, the elements are filtered counting backwards from the last element. So for example, if you filter a collection using `:eq(-1)`, you'll have the same element as if you applied `:last()`.

Keep in mind that the index of a collection starts from 0. So, the first element of the matched collection has index 0, the second element has index 1, and so on. Thus, the Even selector will counter-intuitively choose the odd-positioned elements because of their even indexes. For example, the Even selector will collect the first, third, fifth and so on elements of a collection because they have odd indexes (that is: 0, 2, 4, and so on). In conclusion, remember that Even and Odd are related to the elements' index inside the collection, not their position.

How to do it...

Our goal is to use some of the listed filters. To do that, we'll use a list and apply a red color to the text of the odd-indexed list items having class bold. In addition, we'll hide the first item, and also replace the text of the items with a position greater than 2. To perform these tasks, follow these steps:

1. Create a copy of the `template.html` file and rename it as `position-filters.html`.

2. Inside the `<body>` tag, add the following HTML markup:

    ```html
    <ul>
        <li>First</li>
        <li class="bold">Second</li>
        <li>Third</li>
        <li>Fourth</li>
        <li>Fifth</li>
    </ul>
    ```

3. Edit the `<head>` section of the page adding this code:

    ```html
    <script>
        $(document).ready(function() {
            $('li.bold:odd').css('color', '#FF0A27');
            $('li:first').hide();
            $('li:gt(2)').text('Replaced!');
        });
    </script>
    ```

4. Save the file and open it with your favorite browser.

How it works...

Since these filters are quite simple, also the code has been built to just give you a quick example of what they do. As usual, in the first step we set up a new file using `template.html` as the base file. In second step, we created an unordered list with five elements, with the second item having a bold class. Then, we wrote our little function.

The first selection retrieves all of the `<li>` instances having class bold in the page, and then filters the collection further using the Odd filter to only retain those having an odd index. Once done, it applies a red color to the font using the jQuery's `css()` method. If you already loaded the page, you must have noticed that none of the elements were actually red. This happens because there is just one list item having class bold, so there aren't odd-indexed elements (recalling that the first element has index 0). Thus, the selection returns an empty collection and the style isn't applied at all.

Using the First filter, the second line selects the first element among all of the list items of the page and then hides it. So, since there is just one list in our document, it corresponds to the element having text `First`. In fact, looking at the page you should see just four items instead of the five that we set up.

In the third and last selection, we collect the list items having an index position greater than three (remember the 0-based positioning). Thus, the retrieved nodes are `Fourth` and `Fifth`. Once retrieved, we replace their text with `Replaced!` using the jQuery's `text()` function.

Selecting from elements using filters (Should know)

jQuery has filters that make it easy to select form elements. This section will explain how many, and what are the filters to select those elements.

Getting ready

The filters belonging to this category are as follows:

Name	Description
`:button`	Selects all of the button elements *and* input elements of type button.
`:checkbox`	Selects all of the elements of type `checkbox`.
`:checked`	Selects all of the input elements that are *and* select elements that are selected.
`:disabled`	Selects all of the elements that are disabled.
`:enabled`	Selects all of the elements that are enabled.
`:file`	Selects all of the elements of type `file`.
`:image`	Selects all of the elements of type `image`.
`:input`	Select all of the elements that belong to one of these type: `input`, `select`, `textarea`, and `button`.
`:password`	Selects all of the elements of type `password`.
`:radio`	Selects all of the elements of type `radio`.
`:reset`	Selects all of the elements of type `reset`.
`:selected`	Selects all of the elements that are `selected`.
`:submit`	Selects all of the elements of type `submit`.
`:text`	Selects all of the elements of type `text`.

Please, also consider the following note.

Until few weeks ago, the documentation asserted that :checked selects only checked elements. This was false because it actually selects also option elements that are selected. Proof:

```
return (nodeName === "input" && !!elem.checked) ||
(nodeName === "option" && !!elem.selected);
```

I've sent a pull request (pull #306) for this issue that has been accepted and merged, but if you already know this selector, keep this note in mind.

How to do it...

Wow, there are really a lot of filters belonging to this category. Our goal is to print the selected nodes on the console using some of the listed filters. To do that, follow these steps:

1. Create a copy of the `template.html` file and rename it as `form-filters.html`.

2. Inside the `<body>` tag, add the following HTML markup:

```
<form name="registration-form" id="registration-form"
action="registration.php" method="post">
    <label>Name:</label>
    <input type="text" name="name" placeholder="Name" />
    <label>Surname:</label>
    <input type="text" name="surname" placeholder="Surname" />
    <label>Email:</label>
    <input type="email" name="email" placeholder="Email" />
    <label>Phone:</label>
    <input type="tel" name="phone-number" placeholder="Phone
number" disabled="disabled" />
    <label>Privacy:</label>
    <input name="privacy" type="checkbox" checked="checked" />
    <label>Contact me:</label>
    <input name="contact-me" type="checkbox" />
    <label>Sex:</label>
    <select name="sex">
        <option selected="selected" value="m">Male</option>
        <option value="f">Female</option>
    </select>
    <input type="submit" value="Register" />
</form>
```

3. Edit the `<head>` section of the page adding this code:

```
<script>
    $(document).ready(function() {
        console.log($(':input').length);
        console.log($(':selected').length);
        console.log($('input:disabled').length);
    });
</script>
```

4. Save the file and open it with your favorite browser.

How it works...

After creating the file for this recipe's example, we wrote a form to see our new selectors in action. As always, the third step is reserved to the JavaScript code we're going to analyze. To keep the example simple, the first two lines use implicitly the All selector. As pointed out before, it'll result in lower performance and you should avoid its use in your websites and applications. However, since we have very few nodes, the difference won't be evident.

Once opened, our page will print the following result:

html	body	
8		form-filters.html:17
1		form-filters.html:18
1		form-filters.html:19
>		

Let's understand why.

In the first selection, using the `:input` filter, we collect the elements that belong to one of these type: `input`, `select`, `textarea`, and `button`. Then, we simply print the length of the collection on the console. The selection retrieves 7 `<input>` instances, 1 `<select>`, 0 `<textarea>` instances, and 0 `<button>` instances, and this explains why the first printed length is 8.

On the second line, we collect all of the elements that have the `selected` attribute applied (regardless of its value). Reading the HTML code, it isn't hard to see that the only retrieved element is the option having text "Male", and therefore the second printed line on the console is 1.

The last selection takes advantage of the Element selector to speed up performance and see how filters can be applied to other selectors. Here, we're asking jQuery to select all of the `<input>` elements that have the `disabled` attribute applied (regardless of its value). This time too there is just one match corresponding to the element having label "Phone." Just like the previous statement, printing the `length` property will display the value 1.

Child filters (Should know)

jQuery also has specific filters to target node's children. Here, you'll discover more about them.

Getting ready

The filters belonging to this category are:

Name	Description
`:first-child`	Retrieves the elements that are the first child of their parent.
`:first-of-type`	Collects the elements that are the first of the given type (element name).
`:last-child`	Retrieves the elements that are the last child of their parent.
`:last-of-type`	Collects the elements that are the last of the given type (element name).
`:nth-child()`	Retrieves all elements that are the nth-child of their parent.
`:nth-last-child()`	Selects all elements that are the nth-child of their parent, counting from the last element to the first.
`:nth-last-of-type()`	Selects all elements that are the nth-child of their parent, counting from the last element to the first.
`:nth-of-type()`	Collects all elements that are the nth child of their parent in relation to siblings with the same element name.
`:only-child`	Retrieves all of the elements that are the only child of their parent.
`:only-of-type`	Retrieves the elements that have no siblings with the same element name.

The filters `:nth-child()`, `:nth-last-child()`, `:nth-last-of-type()`, and `:nth-of-type()` accept a selector that can be an index, even, odd, or an equation. Please note that `:nth-last-child()` and `:nth-last-of-type()` use the index starting from the end to turn back.

Besides this, there are some differences between these filters and those we've seen in the *Selecting by position using filters (Should know)* recipe:

 Differently from the :eq() and similar filters, their index starts from one (1) instead of zero (0). Besides, while even and odd are very easy to understand, this isn't the same with equation. The latter is a string having unknown variable as *n*. So, if you want to target the element at position multiple of three (for example 3, 6, 9, and so on), you need to write 3n.

How to do it...

To complete the recipe, follow these steps:

1. Create a copy of the `template.html` file and rename it as `child-filters.html`.

2. Inside the `<body>` tag, add the following HTML markup:

```
<h1 id="title">A great title</h1>
<div class="wrapper">
    <h2>A subtitle</h2>
    <p>This is the first paragraph.</p>
    <p id="description" class="border">I'm a paragraph.</p>
</div>
<div id="content">
    <h2>jQuery is so cool!</h2>
    <p class="border">I'm yet another paragraph</p>
    <ul>
        <li>The first of the list</li>
        <li>I'm the second, not bad!</li>
        <li>Third list item here</li>
        <li>Fourth list item here</li>
        <li>Fifth list item here</li>
    </ul>
    <h2>Another subtitle</h2>
</div>
```

3. Edit the `<head>` section of the page adding this code:

```
<script>
    $(document).ready(function() {
        $('div > h2:first-of-type').css('background-color',
'#976FAC');
        $('li:nth-child(3n+1)').css('color', '#9FB35A');
    });
</script>
```

4. Save the file and open it with your favorite browser.

How it works...

As you can see by looking at the code, the more you read the more our selectors become complex.

In the first line of our recipe, in fact, we're using at the same time the Child selector together with two Element selectors and a Child filter. Our goal is to apply a background color to the `<h2>` instances that are the first child of a `<div>` section. If you open the source with your browser, you can see that the background is applied to all of the `<h2>` instances of the page, but not the one having text Another subtitle. In fact, the latter doesn't match the condition of being the first `<h2>` inside the `<div>` section because it appears after the one having text "jQuery is so cool!."

In the second line, we're targeting the `<li>` instances that are multiples of 3 plus 1 (1, 4, 7, and so on) to change their text color. As you can see, the second line is really interesting because it proves the possibility of using an equation as an index selector. This is a really powerful system since you can not only target multiples of a given number, but also add a specific one, hence the use of the *+1* in our equation. Its use can really simplify your life in several cases, so use it when possible instead of creating a complex loop.

Other filters (Become an expert)

So far, we've seen a plethora of filters, but the good thing is that jQuery has a lot more than that. Here, I'll show the remaining filters that I haven't added to the previous categories.

Getting ready

The filters are as follows:

Name	Description
`:animated`	Selects all of the elements that are in the progress of an animation at the time the selector is run.
`:contains()`	Retrieves the elements that contain the text given. The search is performed among the element itself and all of the descendants.
`:empty`	Collects the elements that have no children (including text nodes).
`:focus`	Select the element that has the focus at the time the selector is run.
`:has()`	Selects elements which contain at least one element that matches the specified selector. The search is performed among all of the descendants, not only the children.
`:header`	Retrieves all of the headers (h1, h2, h3, h4, h5, and h6)

Name	Description
:hidden	Selects all elements that are hidden. An element is considered hidden, not only if it has display: hidden applied, but also if it's physically not shown (for example, if it has width and height set to zero). More on this here: http://api.jquery.com/hidden-selector/.
:lang()	Selects all elements of the specified language.
:not()	Collects the elements that do not match the given selector.
:parent	Selects the elements that have at least one child node (either an element or text).
:root	Retrieves the element which is the root of the document.
:target	Selects the target element indicated by the fragment identifier of the document's URI.
:visible	Selects all elements that are visible. An element is considered visible if it occupies space in the page. So, also if an element has visibility: hidden applied, thus not shown, it's retrieved because it still occupies space. More information is available at http://api.jquery.com/visible-selector/.

How to do it...

To perform the task, follow these steps:

1. Create a copy of the `child-filters.html` file and rename it as `other-filters.html`.

2. Edit the `<head>` section of the page adding this code:

```
<script>
    $(document).ready(function() {
        $('h2:contains(jQuery)').css('background-color',
'#976FAC');
        console.log($('div:has(p.border)').length);
        console.log($('div:not(.wrapper)').length);
    });
</script>
```

3. Save the file, open it with your favorite browser and take a look at the console.

How it works...

In the first line of our anonymous function, we're selecting all of the `<h2>` instances that contain the text jQuery. To achieve this goal, we're relying on the `:contains()` filter passing it to the string we're searching for. Looking at the code, it isn't hard to see that the only element that matches is the first `<h2>` contained in the `<div id="content">` section. Once retrieved, we apply a violet background color to it.

In the second task, we're searching for all of the `<div>` instances that have at least one paragraph which have the class "border" applied. Since both the `<div>` instances of our page have at least one paragraph that matches (precisely both have just one of those paragraphs), the selection retrieves them all. Once done, we print the length of the collection on the console that is **2**.

The last statement collects all of the `<div>` instances that don't have a class wrapper applied. Once again, looking at the HTML source, you can see that the first `<div>` section is the only one having the class applied. So, our selection will only retrieve the second `<div>`, and this explains why the console displays the number **1** in the last line.

Custom filters (Become an expert)

We've learned all of the available jQuery's filters. In some cases you may need a shortcut to collect elements for which jQuery doesn't provide a specific filter. This is exactly where custom filters come into play.

How to do it...

Our goal is to print the length of the elements having the placeholder attribute set, taking advantage of a previously created custom filter. In addition, to see all of the available options in action, we'll create a second filter to collect all of the elements having a name with less than a given number of characters.

To complete the task, follow these steps:

1. Create a copy of the `form-filters.html` file and rename it as `custom-filters.html`.

2. Edit the `<head>` section of the page, replacing the previous custom JavaScript code with this one:

```
<script>
    $.expr[':'].placeholder = function(elem) {
        return $(elem).attr('placeholder') !== undefined;
    };
    $.expr[':'].nameLengthLessThan =
    $.expr.createPseudo(function(filterParam) {
        var length = parseInt(filterParam);
        return function(elem, context, isXml) {
            return $(elem).attr('name') !== undefined &&
            $(elem).attr('name').length < length;
        }
    });
```

```
$(document).ready(function() {
    console.log($(':placeholder').length);
    console.log($('input:nameLengthLessThan(5)').length);
});
</script>
```

3. Save the file and open it with your favorite browser.

How it works...

At the very beginning of our JavaScript instructions for this page, we've added a property, or more specifically a function called `placeholder` to the : (yes, it's a property called colon, you read it right) attribute that belongs to the jQuery's `expr` attribute. : is a property containing jQuery's native filters and you can use it to add your own at runtime. Inside the function definition, we just have a single statement that checks if the current element has the `placeholder` attribute set, and if so, it returns true to keep the element.

As you can see from the example, in this basic version, a filter is nothing but a function that accepts as an argument the current DOM element to process and needs to return `true` to keep it in the collection, and `false` to discard it. You should use this method when the following are true:

▸ you're interested only in the element to process itself

▸ the filter doesn't accept an argument

▸ the context to which the selection is applied doesn't matter

The second custom filter, called `nameLengthLessThan`, is slightly more complicated and uses the method introduced (and encouraged) starting from jQuery 1.8. To the `createPseudo` function we pass an anonymous function having a parameter that represents the argument passed to the filter when you use it. Inside it, we create another function that will be returned and that is responsible to perform the filtering. To the latter, jQuery passes the element to be processed (`elem` parameter), the DOMElement or DOMDocument from which selection will occur (`context` parameter), and a Boolean that tells if you're operating on an XML document. As you may guess, for this filter we need this pattern because our filter needs to know the limit of characters the `name` attribute of the element must comply with. In other words, we need to pass the number of characters the value of the `name` attribute must respect.

Inside the inner-most function, we write the code to test if the element should be kept or not, for our example, this means checking whether the `name` attribute is set and its length is not less than the given length (stored using a closure inside the `length` variable).

Now that we've created the filters, we need to use it. Inside the handler for the `document.ready` event, there are two statements. The first calls the `placeholder` filter without parameters and using implicitly the Universal selector. The second uses the `nameLengthLessThan` filter passing 5 as parameter and using the Element selector. Using the Element selector in the second call will result in a performance improvement. The execution of our code will result, as expected, in the following lines printed on the console:

4

1

Context matters (Should know)

So far I've mentioned vaguely something called context that can be used during a selection. This recipe illustrates how and why we use the second parameter of jQuery, *context*.

How to do it...

Our goal is to apply a border to all of the `<li>` descendants of an element having ID content, using the context parameter. Perform the following steps:

1. Create a copy of the `child-filters.html` file and rename it as `context-matters.html`.

2. Edit the `<head>` section of the page adding this code:

```
<script>
    $(document).ready(function() {
        $('li', '#content').css('border', '2px solid #000000');
    });
</script>
```

3. Save the file and open it with your favorite browser.

How it works...

This recipe is very simple because I want you to focus on the consequences of using the second parameter of the constructor. In the only statement inside the anonymous function, we've passed two arguments to the constructor. The first is the usual selector, while the second, `context`, can be a DOM element, the document, or a jQuery object and acts as an ancestor. So, in our example, we retrieved the `<li>` elements descendants of the element having id `content` and then applied a solid black border with 2px width.

There's more...

We've already seen how we can combine multiple selectors to create a more complex one. To achieve the goal of this recipe using your current knowledge, you should have thought of a selector like the following:

```
$('#context li')
```

If you did, give me five! This selector would do the job, but there's a more efficient way. Before talking about performance, let's discover a little more.

What exactly is `context`? By default, jQuery performs searches within the DOM starting from the document root. The framework splits the selector into multiple parts and then processes them, but this process is usually slower than the one using `context`. The latter is used to restrict the searches to one or more subtrees, depending on the selector used, that usually will result in a performance improvement.

When you use the second argument, what jQuery does is to firstly retrieve elements based on the `context` selector and then collects the descendants that match the first parameter, `selector`. The second argument helps a lot in case where you have a very large DOM and the selector you're using really narrow down the subtree(s) where it'll perform the second phase of the search.

The most observant of you may guess why I talked about ancestor and not parent. The answer is simple and comes directly from the source. In fact, behind the scenes, the framework uses the `find()` method that, starting from an elements' collection, searches for descendants that match a given selector. The proof is the following snippet taken from the source:

```
// HANDLE: $(expr, context)
// (which is just equivalent to: $(context).find(expr)
} else {
    return this.constructor( context ).find( selector );
}
```

As I said, the use of `context` doesn't always boost performance. For example, if you're selecting an element by its id, you won't have any benefits. Thus:

```
$('#someId', 'p')
```

won't improve performance compared to:

```
$('#someId')
```

Indeed, the first solution slows down the selection because it firstly needs to retrieve a potentially high number of paragraphs and then test their descendants, instead of taking advantage of the native `getElementById()`.

Where it can really make a difference is when `selector` is searching for a tag name or a class, or when context is an ID. Thus, a selection like the following:

```
$('#aDiv .red')
```

can be turned into this:

```
$('.red', '#aDiv')
```

One important point to keep in mind is that when it comes to performance, there isn't a rule that is always true. It really depends on several factors, like how many and what are the nodes of your DOM, and the browser. So, the best advice I can give is to test your selectors and see what's the best solution by applying the knowledge you're (hopefully) acquiring reading this book.

Improving performance re-using selected elements (Become an expert)

In this recipe, we'll see how we can store a collection of previously selected elements in a variable for a later processing and how this method can improve performance.

How to do it...

This time our goal will be a little different. Instead of applying margins or borders, we'll perform a comparison to show how in a (simulation of a) real-world page, caching objects can significantly improve performance. In order to understand the explanation, follow these steps:

1. Create a copy of the `template.html` file and rename it as `reusing-elements.html`.

2. Edit the `<head>` section of the page adding this code:

```
<script>
    $(document).ready(function() {
        var start = new Date();
        var $description = $('.description');
        for (i = 0; i < 50000; i++) {
            $description.text();
        }
        console.log('Time with caching: ' + (new Date() -
            start) + ' milliseconds');
        start = new Date();
        for (i = 0; i < 50000; i++) {
            $('.description').text();
        }
    }
```

```
        console.log('Time without caching: ' + (new Date()
            - start) + ' milliseconds');
    });
</script>
```

3. Save the file and open it with your favorite browser.

How it works...

Basically, our code can be split into two blocks. Their general goal is to retrieve all of the elements with class "description" and then call the jQuery's `text()` method a given number of times (50,000 in our example). The difference is that while the first retrieves the collection once, stores it into a variable and then calls `text()` inside the loop, the second calls the constructor inside the loop as well. Of course, it's unlikely that you'll call a constructor so many times inside your code, but the demo wants to stress on the performance difference that a simple caching can make.

Before each loop, we save the current time in milliseconds using the JavaScript `Date` class in a variable called `start`. Then, right after the loop, we print the elapsed time on the console. The difference between the two blocks is quietly impressive, and is shown by the following table:

	Test #1	Test #2	Test #3	Average
Time with caching	18 ms	17 ms	17 ms	17,3 ms
Time without caching	227 ms	216 ms	224 ms	222,3 ms
	(more than 209 ms)	(more than 199 ms)	(more than 207 ms)	(more than 205 ms)
	Approximately 11, 5x slower	Approximately 11x slower	Approxiamtely 11, 5x slower	Approxiamtely 11, 5x slower

 While a rough benchmark can be done using the `Date` class, a more reliable one should be performed with the **High Resolution Time** API. You can find more information on this API reading this article of mine at `http://www.sitepoint.com/discovering-the-high-resolution-time-api/`.

From this recipe, we can learn a good rule of thumb: if we're going to use a selector at least twice, we should cache it. Then, when you need to call it again, you'll just use the variable where you stored the collection. Doing so, jQuery won't need to search the entire DOM tree again to find the elements, which leads to better performance.

Some of you may argue that the example shown couldn't be seen as a real use case. For those of you, the following is a piece of code taken directly from the current version of my website. The aim of this snippet is to rotate my latest tweets, but this doesn't really matter. What I want you to focus is the way I cached the collection of elements having class `tweet` inside the variable called `$tweets` and then reused it many times, especially in the anonymous function:

```
// Rotate the latest tweets
var $tweets = $('.tweet');
$tweets.not(':first-child').hide();
window.setInterval(
    function () {
        $tweets
            .filter(':visible')
            .fadeOut('slow', 'linear', function () {
                var $next = $(this).next($tweets.selector);
                if ($next.length === 0) {
                    $next = $tweets.first();
                }
                $next.fadeIn('slow', 'linear');
            });
    },
    5000
);
```

Methods to filter collections (Become an expert)

We've already delved into filters, but what you probably don't know is that jQuery has methods to filter collections as well. This section describes how many and what are these methods.

Getting ready

The methods of this type are:

Name	Description
eq()	Reduces the retrieved collection to the element having position index+1.
filter()	Reduces the collection to those elements that match the given selector or pass the test function.
first()	Keeps just the first element of the collection.
has()	Reduces the set of matched elements to those that have a descendant that matches the selector or DOM element.

Name	Description
last()	Keeps just the last element of the collection.
map()	Each element of the collection is passed to the given function and only those that are returned are kept.
not()	Removes the collection's elements that match the given selector.
slice()	Reduces the retrieved collection to those elements having a position within a specified range.

Also consider the following note:

The jQuery documentation includes also the is() method in this category, but I didn't because its aim isn't to filter a collection, but to test it. In fact, citing the documentation, the is() method Checks the current matched set of elements against a selector, element, or jQuery object and return true if at least one of these elements matches the given arguments.

How to do it...

This recipe will show you the use of some of the cited methods:

1. Create a copy of the `hierarchy-selectors.html` file and rename it as `filter-methods.html`.

2. Edit the <head> section of the page adding this code:

```
<script>
    $(document).ready(function() {
        console.log($('p.border').eq(-1).text());
        console.log($('div').has('ul').length);
        console.log(
            $('div').map(function(index, domElem) {
                if ($('#note', domElem).length !== 0) {
                    return domElem;
                }
            })
            .length
        );
    });
</script>
```

3. Save the file and open it with your favorite browser.

How it works...

This recipe uses three of the eight methods described. Before talking about what our code does, it's worth noting that at this point of the book, some of them should be really familiar. In fact, we've already met filters called `:eq`, `:first`, `:last` and `:not`. Surprisingly, the methods having the same name, but do not act like their respective filters.

On opening the created file on your browser, you should see the following lines on the console:

I'm yet another paragraph

1

1

Let's discover why we have this output.

In the first line of our function we selected all of the paragraphs having the class border applied and then filtered using the `eq()` method. As you can see, it shows the use of `eq()` using a negative index that, as I already pointed out in the *Selecting by position using filters (Should know)* recipe, lets the count start from the end of the collection. We passed -1, which means we're selecting the last element of the collection. In our code there are just two paragraphs that match, but since we're choosing only the last, our final collection contains only the paragraph having text I'm yet another paragraph. Once filtered, we print on the console the text of the node using the `text()` method and this explains the first line of the resulting output.

The following statement selects all of the `<div>` instances of the page but keeps only those having a `<ul>` as descendant. The filter is achieved using the `has()` method described in the previous table. After that, we print on the console the length of the retrieved collection that is composed by just one element as you can confirm looking at the HTML code.

The third and last statement, are the more complex ones. We start again selecting all of the `<div>` instances of the page, but this time we reduce the set of matched elements using `map()`. The latter iterates over the collection elements and accepts a callback function which can take up to two arguments: the index of the current element and the element itself. Besides, within the callback function, `this` refers to the current DOM element. Its basic use is to return the element if you want to keep it, and `null` or `undefined` (no return is the same as returning `undefined`) to remove it. However, you can also return an array of data items to be inserted into the resulting set.

As a callback, we're using an anonymous function. Inside it we test if the current node has a descendant having ID `note`, in which case we keep the element by returning it. Once the entire collection is processed, we write the length of the new one on the console. This time too, you can see that the console shows the right value.

Traversing DOM SubTrees (Become an expert)

Now that the book is almost at its end, you should be convinced of the jQuery's power. However, I can guarantee that we've touched only the tip of the iceberg because with jQuery you can really, really do more than that.

This section describes how many, and what are the methods that can be applied to a collection to find elements starting from a matched set. One of these methods is `find()`; we have come across it several times.

Getting ready

The Tree Traversal methods are:

Name	Description
`children()`	Retrieves the children of every element in the previously created collection. If a selector is passed, only the children that match it are retrieved.
`closest()`	Gets the first element that matches the given selector for every element in the collection. The search is performed starting from the element itself and then traversing up through its ancestors in the DOM tree.
`find()`	Picks up the descendants of each element in the collection that match the given, mandatory selector.
`next()`	Collect the immediately following sibling of each element in the set of matched elements. It can optionally take a selector, in which case only the next sibling that matches is taken.
`nextAll()`	For each collection's element retrieves the following siblings, optionally filtered by a selector.
`nextUntil()`	Similar to `nextAll()`, but it stops before the element matched by the selector.
`offsetParent()`	Gets the closest ancestor element that is *positioned*. An element is *positioned* if it has a CSS position attribute of relative, absolute, or fixed.
`parent()`	For every element in the previously created collection, gets the parent. It can optionally accept a selector.
`parents()`	Similar to `parent()` but it collects all of the ancestors, not just the parent. It optionally accepts a selector to filter the nodes by testing whether they match it.
`parentsUntil()`	Selects the ancestors of each element in the collection, up to but not including the element matched by the selector.

Name	Description
prev()	Collects the immediately preceding sibling of each element in the collection. It can optionally accept a selector.
prevAll()	For every element in the previously created collection, gets all preceding siblings. It can optionally accept a selector.
prevUntil()	Similar to prevAll(), but it stops before the element matched by the selector.
siblings()	Gets the siblings of each element in the set of matched elements, optionally filtered by a selector.

How to do it...

As you can see, there are a lot of methods belonging to this category. In the following recipe, I'll show you the use of two of them of different type so that you can strongly fix the concepts in your mind.

To build the example, follow these steps:

1. Create a copy of the template.html file and rename it as traversing-methods. html.

2. Inside the <body> tag, add the following HTML markup:

```
<div id="grandfather">
    <div id="father">
        <div id="child-1" class="child">I'm the child of
        #father!</div>
        <div id="child-2" class="child">
            I'm the second child of #father
            <div id="descendant">What a great hierarchy!</div>
        </div>
    </div>
    <div class="uncle">
        First uncle here!
    </div>
    <div class="uncle">
        Second uncle
    </div>
    <div class="uncle">
        Yet another uncle
    </div>
</div>
```

3. Edit the `<head>` section adding the following code just after the `<title>` tag:

```
<style>
    .child {
        background-color: #ED9566;
    }
    .uncle {
        background-color: #66ED66;
    }
    #descendant {
        background-color: #E01B5D;
    }
</style>
```

4. Edit the `<head>` section of the page adding this code:

```
<script>
    $(document).ready(function() {
        $('#grandfather').find('.child').css('margin-left',
'40px');
        var $ancestors = $('#descendant').parents();
        for(var i = 0; i < $ancestors.length; i++) {
            console.log('Element ' + $ancestors[i].tagName +
            ' with id ' + $ancestors[i].id);
        }
    }
</script>
```

5. Save the file and open it with your favorite browser.

How to do it...

In the first line of the anonymous function, we first selected the element having id grandfather and then used the `find()` method to search, among its descendants, those having the class child applied. Looking at our code, you can see that we retrieved two `<div>` instances, the first having ID `child-1` and the second with ID `child-2`. Once retrieved, we applied a left margin of 40px to them so, when opening the file in your browser, you should see these elements shifted from the left side of the page.

The goal of the next block, that is slightly more complex than the previous, is to print on the console the tag name and the id of the ancestors of the element with ID descendant. To perform this task, in the second line we selected the element relying on its id and then, using the `parents()` method, we retrieved its ancestors. Once done, we cached the collection in a variable called `$ancestors` to improve performances.

Then, we created a loop to iterate over the ancestors and print on the console the tag name and the id of each element. Now, you should wonder why I chose to print also the tag name and not only the id. The reason is that we used the `parents()` method, so the collection includes elements such as `<body>` and `<html>` that do not have an id. Therefore, if we printed only the ID, we wouldn't be able to recognize the iterated element. On the contrary, looking at the console, you should see the following output:

```
Element DIV with id child-2
Element DIV with id father
Element DIV with id grandfather
Element BODY with id
Element HTML with id
```

How to have efficient selectors (Become an expert)

Throughout the book, I've given several hints to improve performances. This recipe will reinforce some of them and add other useful tips and tricks to improve the performance of your website by simply selecting elements in the right way.

How to do it...

To boost the performances, keep in mind the following points:

1. Don't use the Universal selector (explicitly or implicitly). Never! Seriously!

2. The best selectors are the Id, Class and Element selectors, because under the hood jQuery uses native JavaScript functions.

3. The best performances are achieved using the ID selector.

4. Never prepend a tag name before an id, it'll slow down the selector. For example, don't turn `$('#content')` into `$('div#content')`.

5. If your selection needs more than one selector, start with the Id selector if possible. For example, `$('#content p.border')`.

6. Remember to use the context parameter or the `find()` method when possible. For example, turn `$('#content p.border')` into `$('p.border', '#content')` or equivalently (as discussed in the *Context Matters should know* recipe) into `$('#content').find('p.border')`.

7. jQuery's selectors engine, called `Sizzle`, parses selectors from right to left. Therefore, to speed up your selection, be more specific on the right part and less on the left. For example, turn `$('div.wrapper .border')` into `$('.wrapper p.border')`.

8. Don't be too specific if the same set can be selected with less selectors. For example, `$('#content p.border')` is better than `$('#content div.wrapper div p.border')`.

9. If you need to use a filter, it's always better to narrow down the set of elements and then use the filter. For example, turn `$(':enabled')` into `$('#formId').find(':enabled')` or even better `$('#formId').find('input:enabled')`.

10. Filters such as, `:button`, `:checkbox`, `:visible`, `:input`, and others are a jQuery extension and not part of the CSS specification, so they can't take advantage of the performance provided by `querySelectorAll()`. To have better performance, it's better to first select elements using a pure CSS selector and then filter using `filter()` (that is, `.filter(':input')`).

11. Filters such as, `:image`, `:text`, `:password`, `:reset` and others are a jQuery extension and not part of the CSS specification, so they can't take advantage of the performance provided by `querySelectorAll()`. To have better performance, it's better to select using the attribute selector. For example, turn `$(':reset')` into `$('[type=reset]')`.

12. To improve the performance of the Not Equal attribute selector in browsers that support `querySelectorAll()`, use the `not()` method. For example, turn `$('.border [placeholder!=Age]')` into `$('.border').not('[placeholder=Age]')`.

13. To improve the performance of `:lt()` filter in modern browsers, use the `slice()` method. For example, turn `$('.border:lt(2)')` into `$('.border').slice(0, 3)`.

14. To improve the performance of the `:gt()` filter in modern browsers, use the `slice()` method. For example, turn `$('.border:gt(2)')` into `$('.border').slice(3)`.

15. To improve the performance of the `:has()` filter in modern browsers, use the `has()` method. For example, turn `$('div:has(p.border)')` into `$('div').has('p.border')`.

About Packt Publishing

Packt, pronounced 'packed', published its first book "*Mastering phpMyAdmin for Effective MySQL Management*" in April 2004 and subsequently continued to specialize in publishing highly focused books on specific technologies and solutions.

Our books and publications share the experiences of your fellow IT professionals in adapting and customizing today's systems, applications, and frameworks. Our solution based books give you the knowledge and power to customize the software and technologies you're using to get the job done. Packt books are more specific and less general than the IT books you have seen in the past. Our unique business model allows us to bring you more focused information, giving you more of what you need to know, and less of what you don't.

Packt is a modern, yet unique publishing company, which focuses on producing quality, cutting-edge books for communities of developers, administrators, and newbies alike. For more information, please visit our website: www.packtpub.com.

Writing for Packt

We welcome all inquiries from people who are interested in authoring. Book proposals should be sent to author@packtpub.com. If your book idea is still at an early stage and you would like to discuss it first before writing a formal book proposal, contact us; one of our commissioning editors will get in touch with you.

We're not just looking for published authors; if you have strong technical skills but no writing experience, our experienced editors can help you develop a writing career, or simply get some additional reward for your expertise.

jQuery for Designers: Beginner's Guide

ISBN: 978-1-84951-670-9   Paperback: 332 pages

An approachable introduction to web design in jQuery for non-programmers

1. Enhance the user experience of your site by adding useful jQuery features

2. Learn the basics of adding impressive jQuery effects and animations even if you've never written a line of JavaScript

3. Easy step-by-step approach shows you everything you need to know to get started improving your website with jQuery

Instant jQuery UI Starter

ISBN: 978-1-78216-823-2   Paperback: 46 pages

Discover how you can create rich end-user experiences for your web applications with jQuery UI

1. Learn something new in an Instant! A short, fast, focused guide delivering immediate results.

2. Learn how you can effectively utilize jQuery UI!

3. Refresh your JavaScript and jQuery skills

4. Quickly create Widgets and interactions

Please check **www.PacktPub.com** for information on our titles